ludovico einaudi

cinema

T0057216

Photographs by Ludovico Einaudi

ISBN 978-1-7051-3804-5

CHESTER MUSIC
part of **WiseMusic**Group

EXCLUSIVELY DISTRIBUTED BY
HAL•LEONARD®

Contact us:
Hal Leonard
7777 West Bluemound Road
Milwaukee, WI 53213
Email: info@halleonard.com

In Europe, contact:
Hal Leonard Europe Limited
42 Wigmore Street
Marylebone, London, W1U 2RN
Email: info@halleonardeurope.com

In Australia, contact:
Hal Leonard Australia Pty. Ltd.
4 Lentara Court
Cheltenham, Victoria, 3192 Australia
Email: info@halleonard.com.au

contents

Experience

Ludovico Einaudi

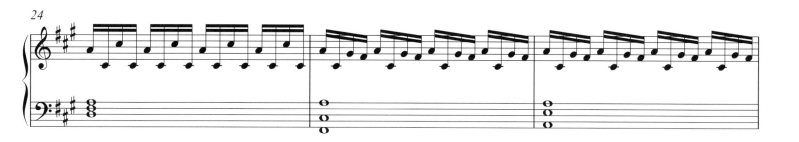

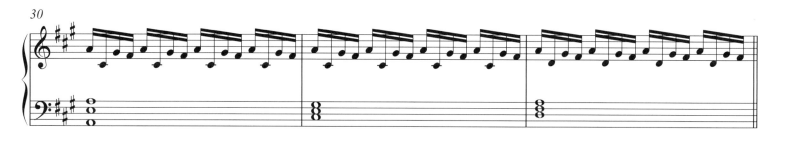

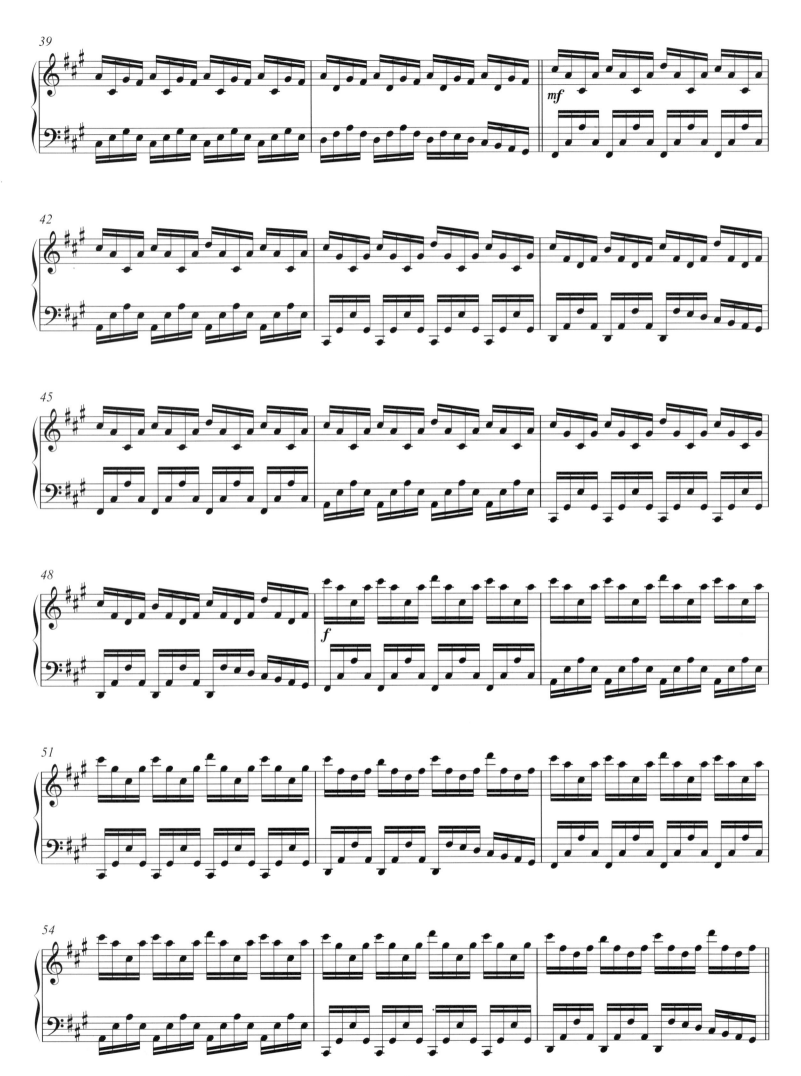

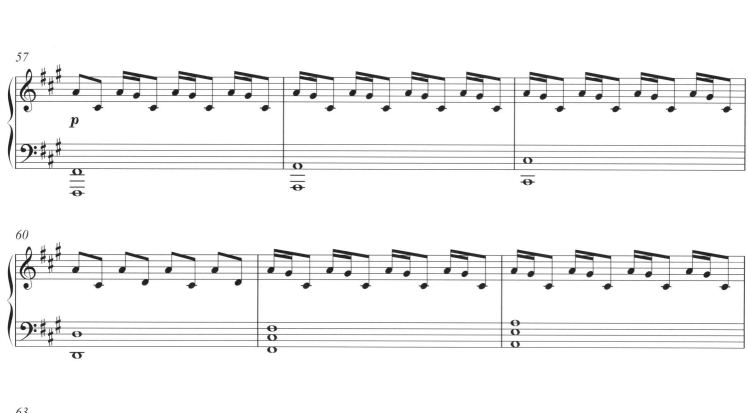

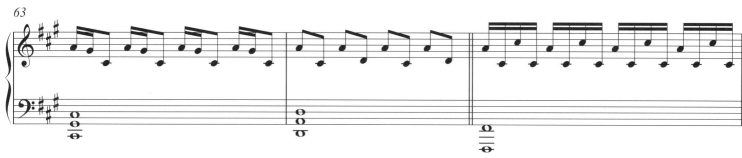

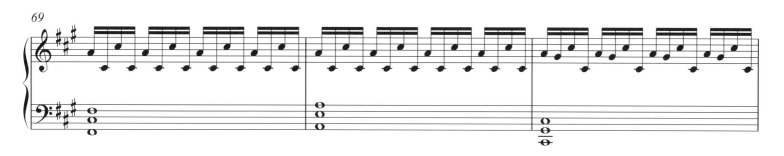

Golden Butterflies

from SEVEN DAYS WALKING: DAY 1

LUDOVICO EINAUDI

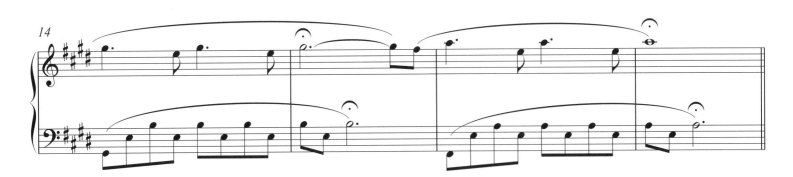

Fluente, senza rubato ♩ = c. 132

mp

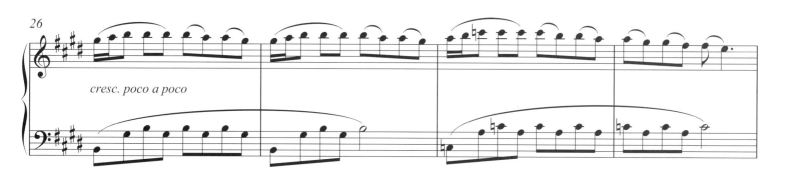

cresc. poco a poco

mf

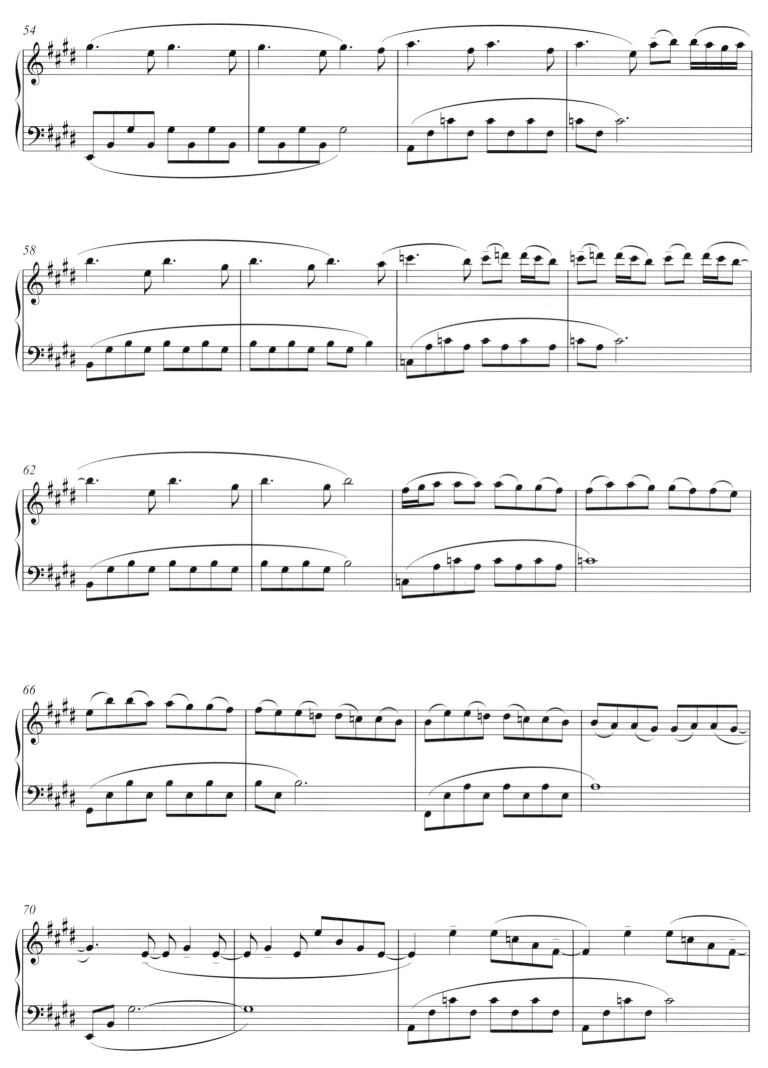

13

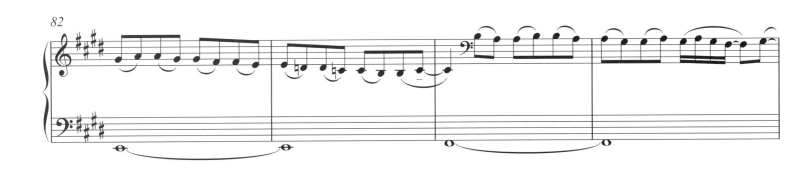

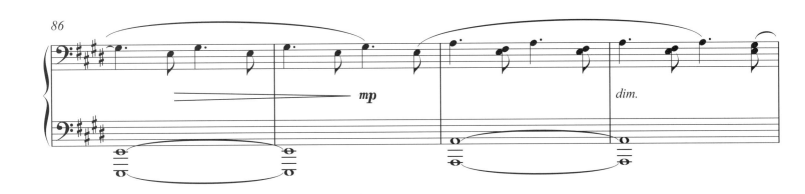

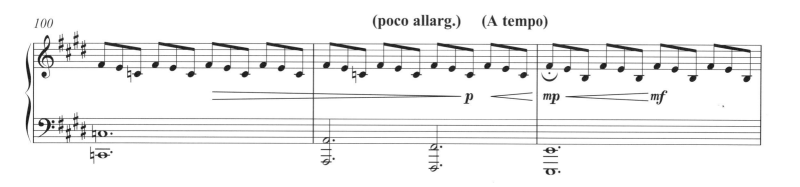

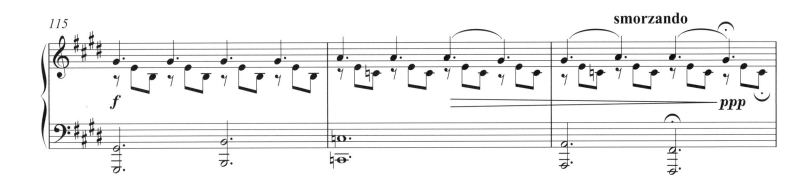

più largo

like bells

ancora più largo

18

Berlin Song

Ludovico Einaudi

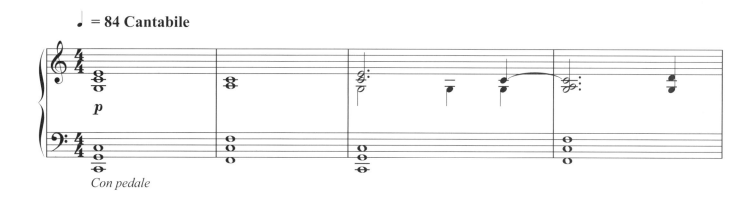

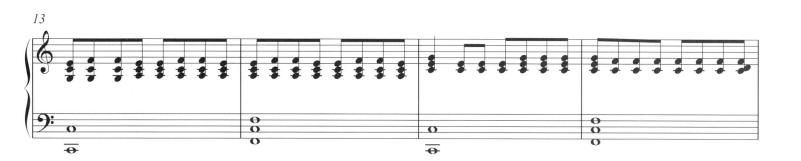

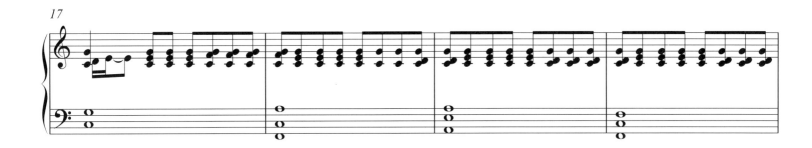

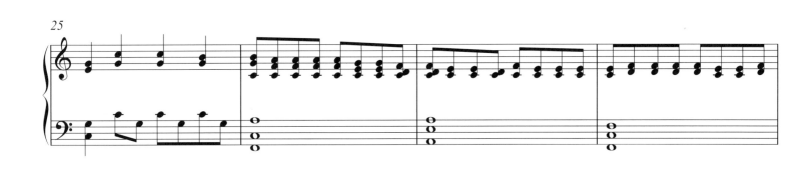

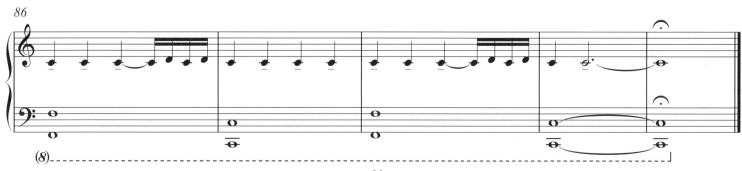

Love Is A Mystery

Ludovico Einaudi

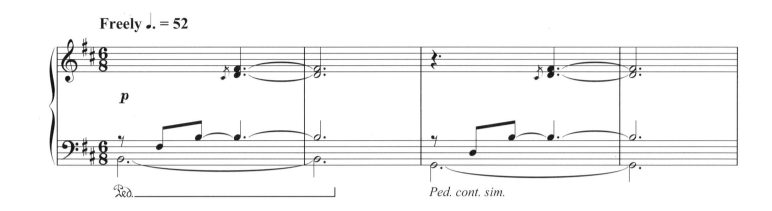

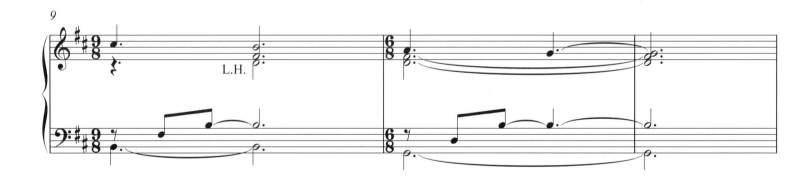

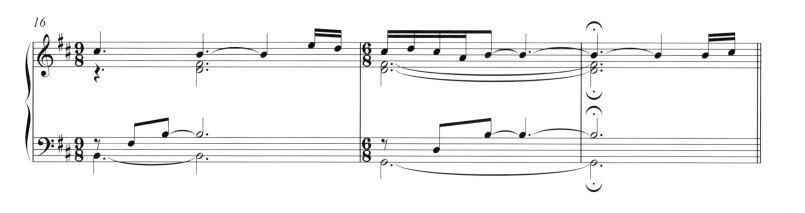

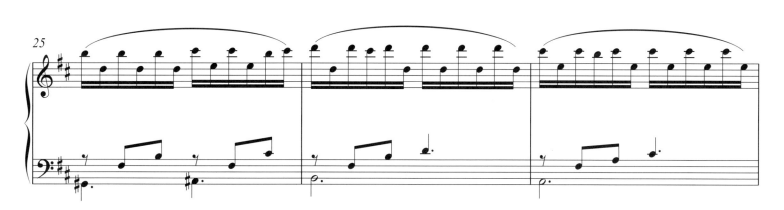

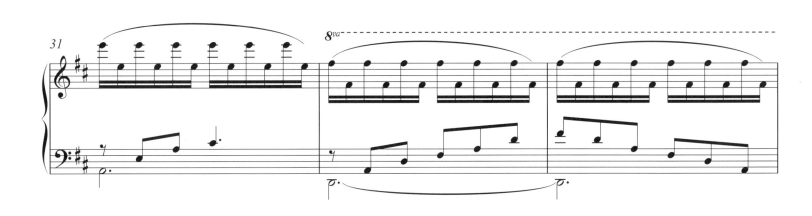

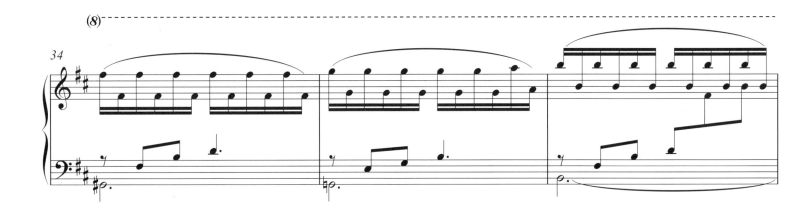

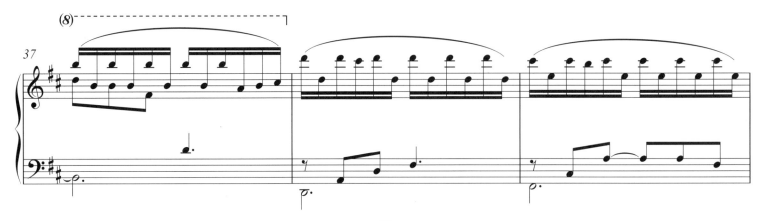

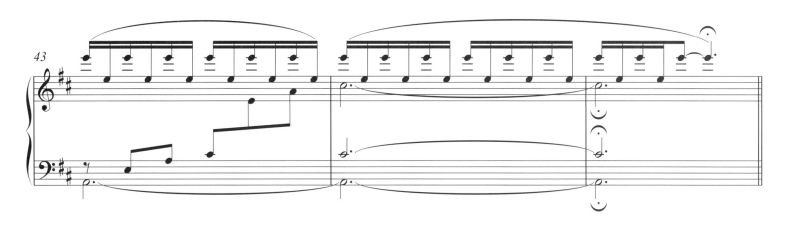

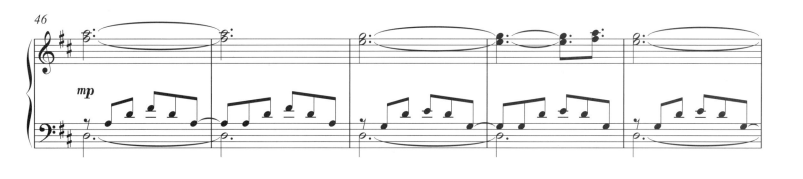

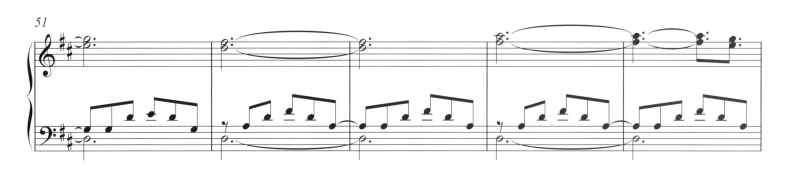

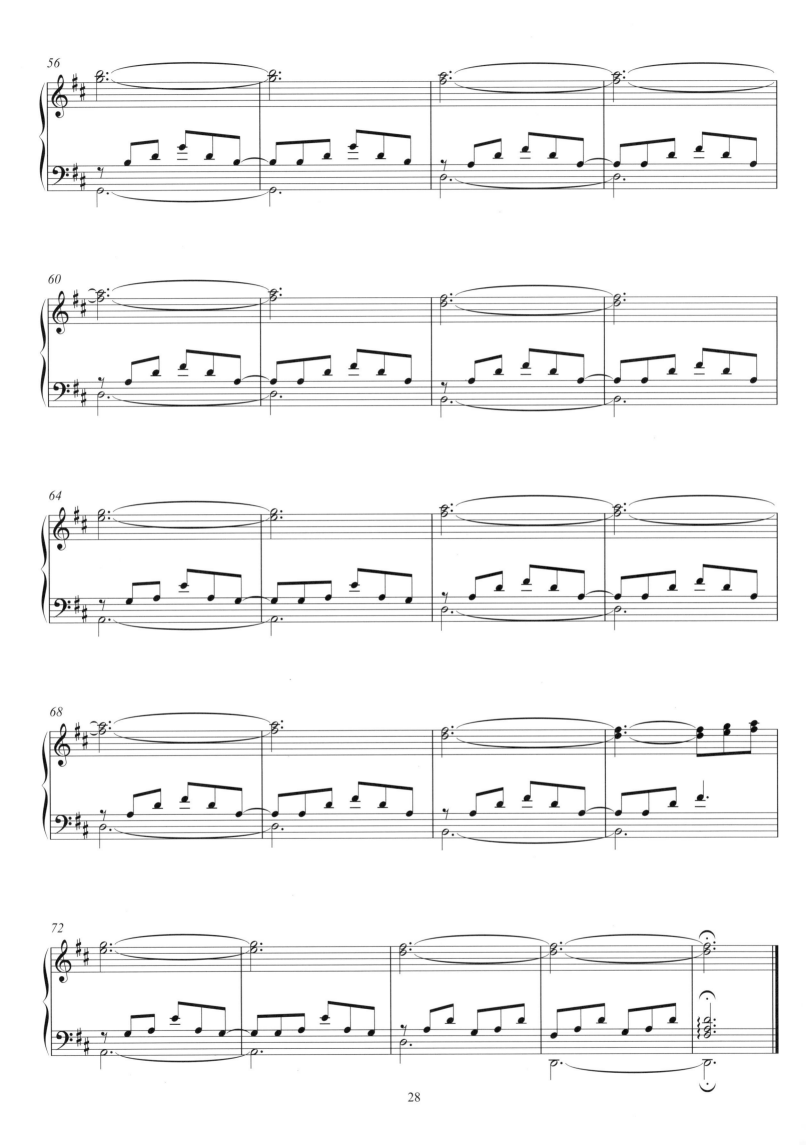

The Water Diviner

Ludovico Einaudi

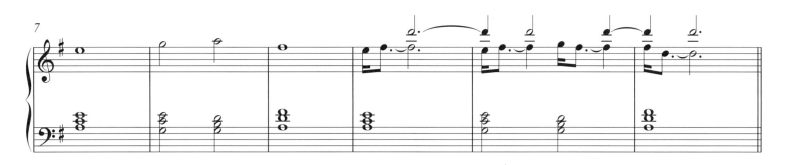

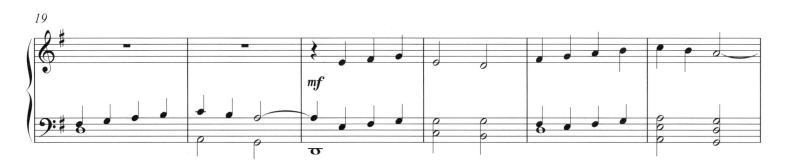

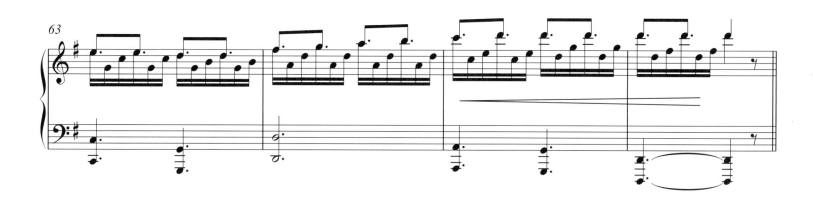

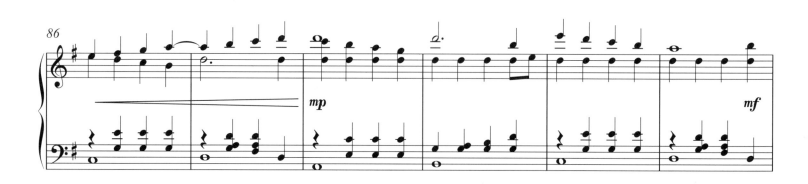

The Third Murder

Ludovico Einaudi

Easy waltz, expressively

With pedal

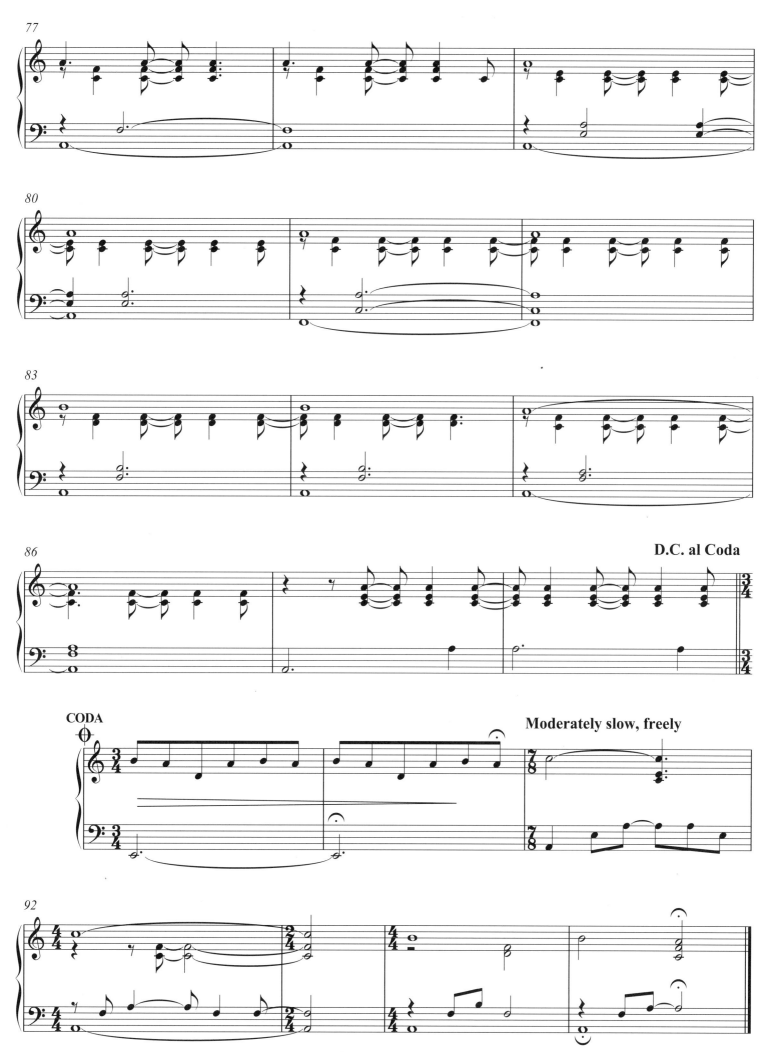

Petricor

Ludovico Einaudi

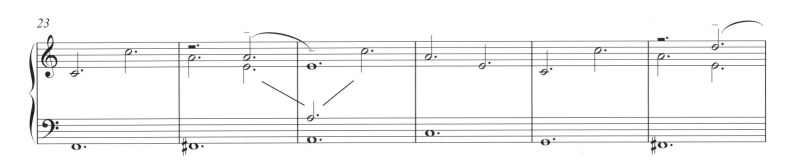

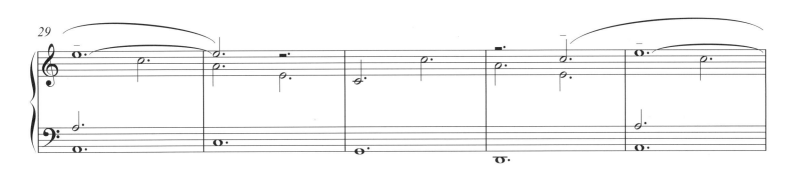

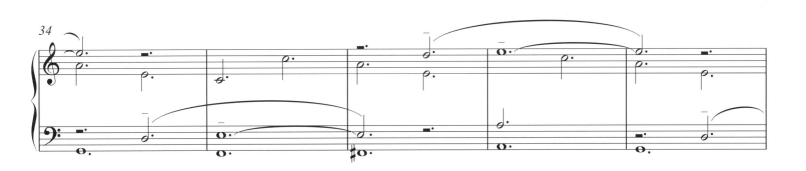

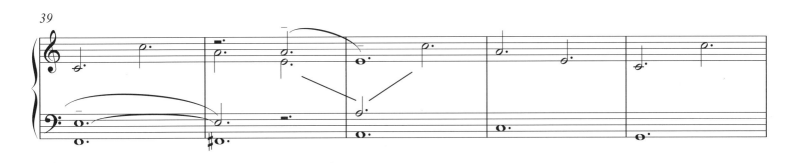

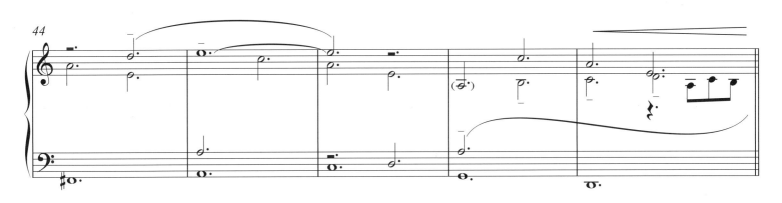

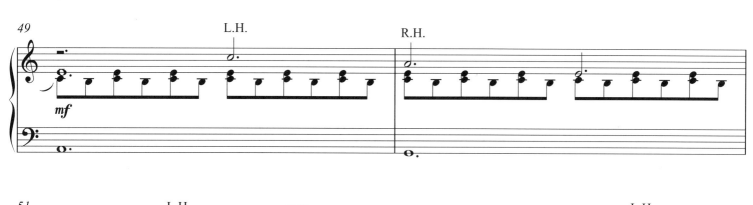

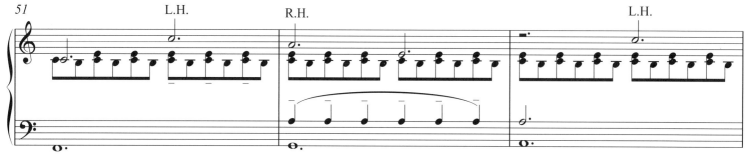

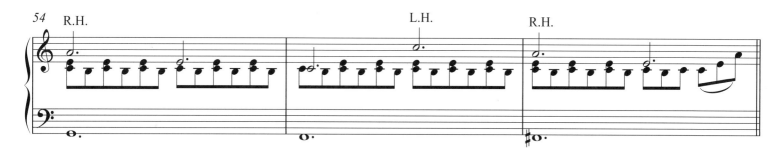

Con brio, l'istesso tempo

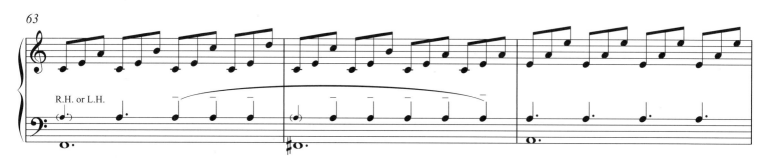

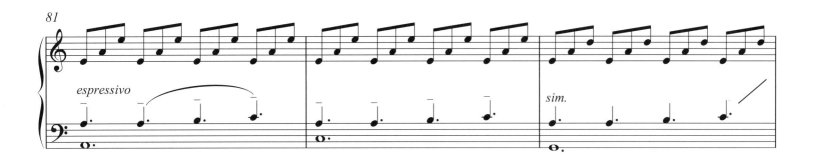

Calmo, l'istesso tempo

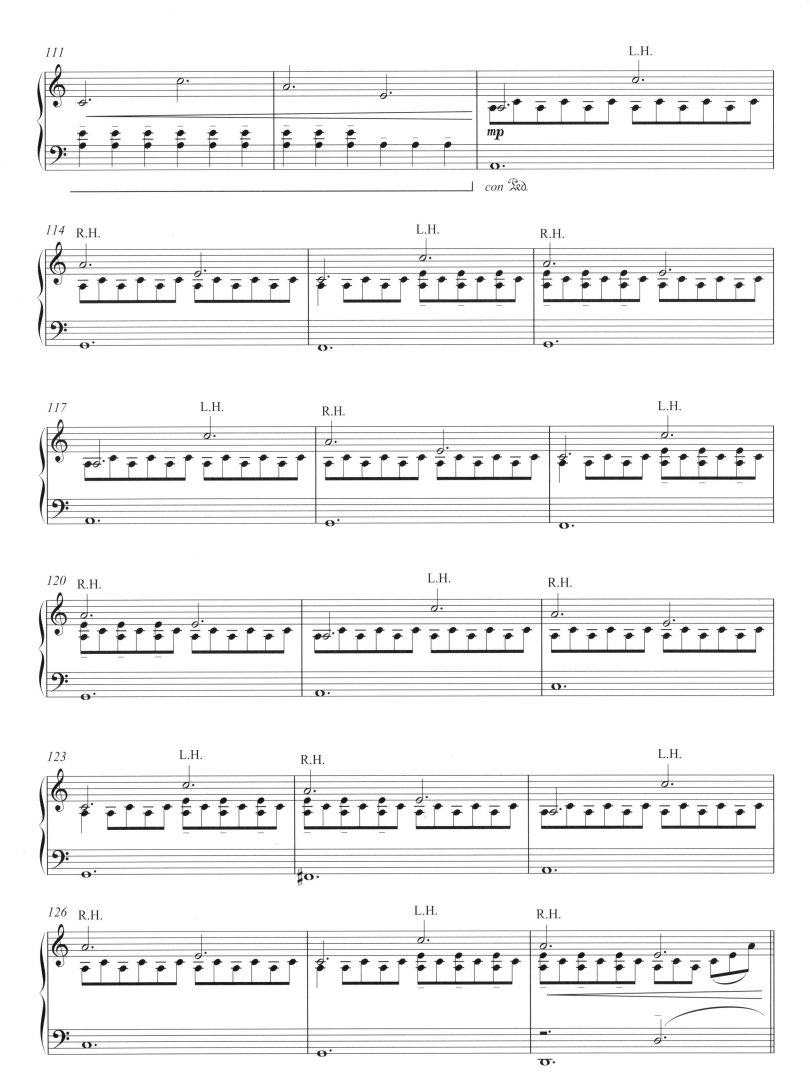

Con brio, l'istesso tempo

Calmo, l'istesso tempo

Fly

Ludovico Einaudi

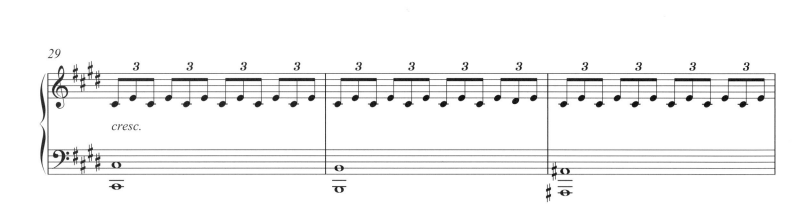

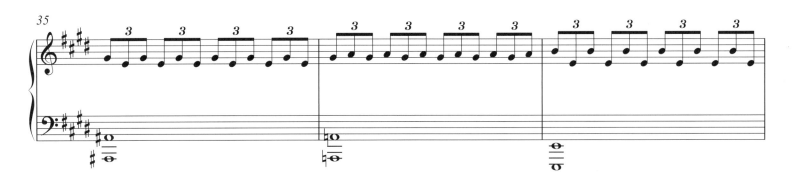

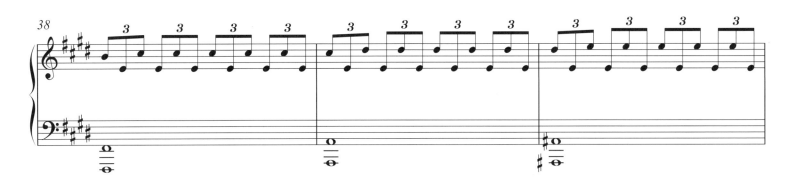

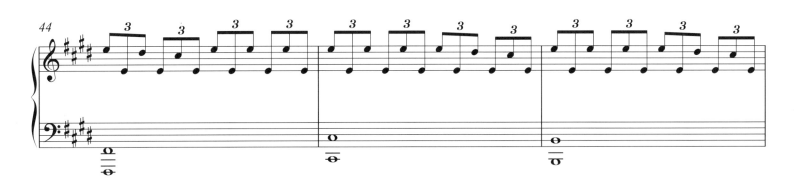

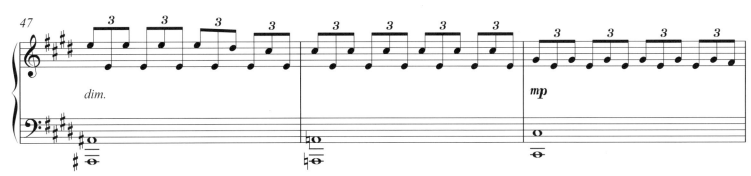

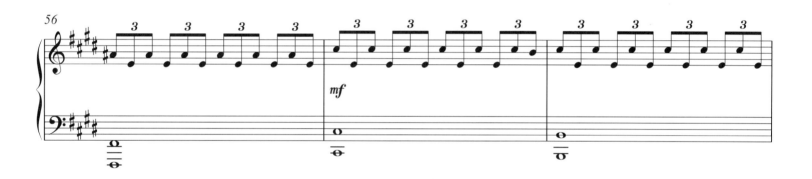

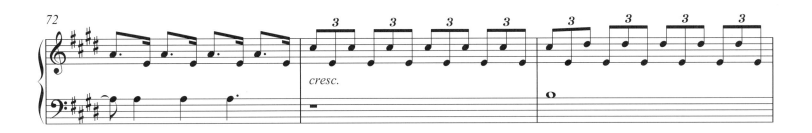

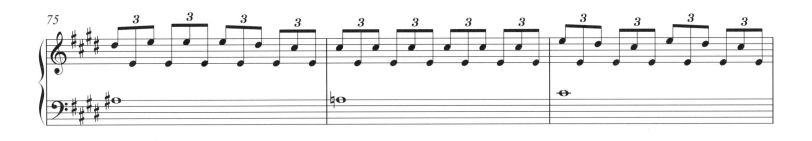

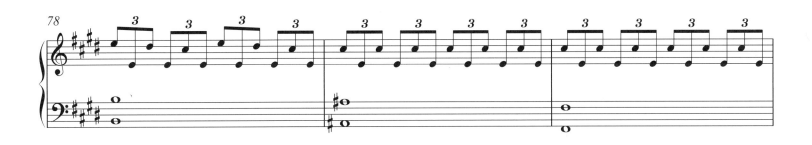

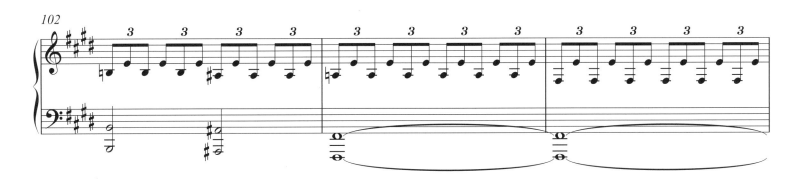

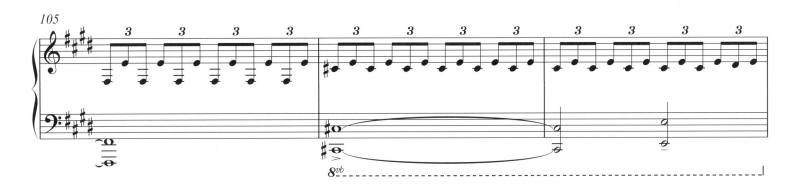

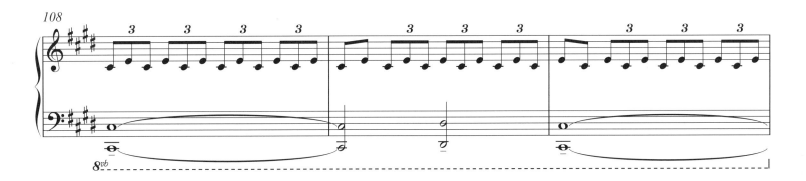

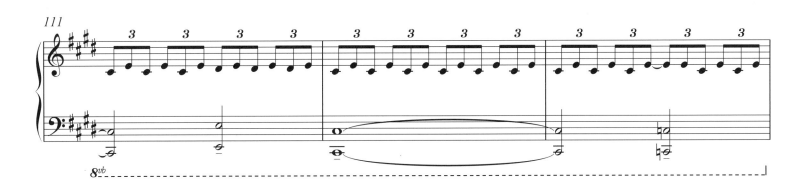

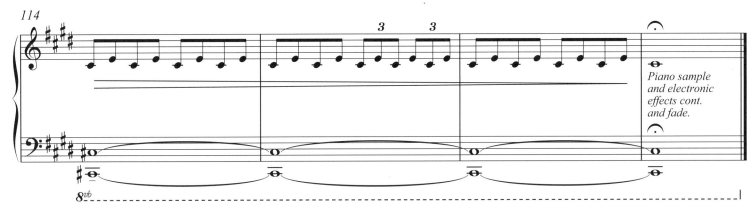

Piano sample and electronic effects cont. and fade.

Time Lapse

Ludovico Einaudi

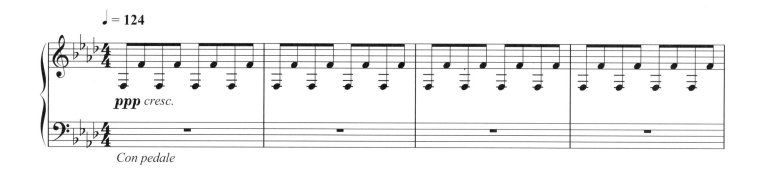

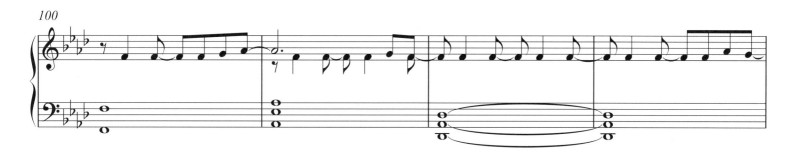

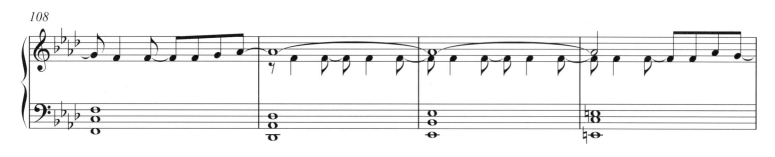

Repeat to fade

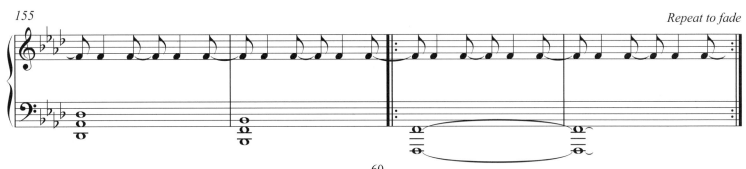

Walk

Ludovico Einaudi

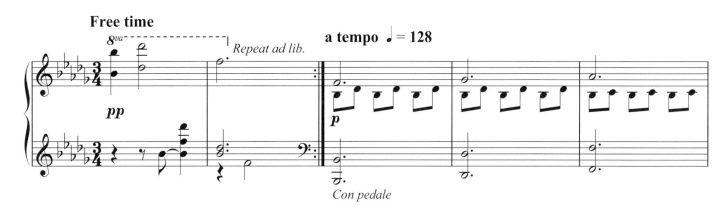

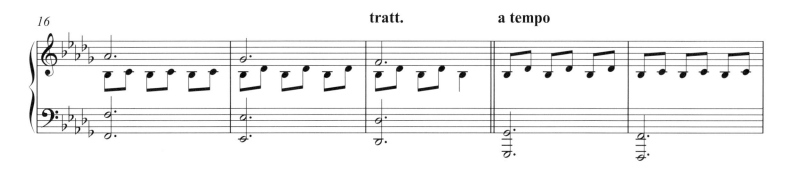

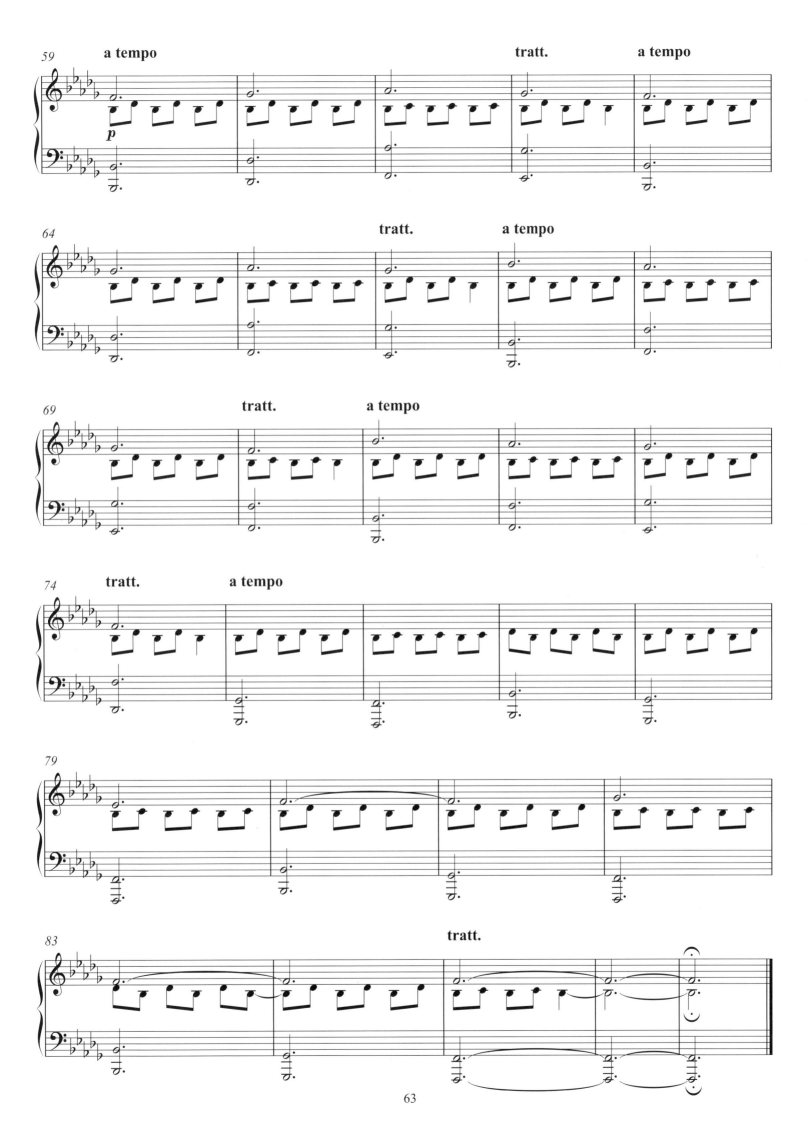

Cold Wind Var. 1

from SEVEN DAYS WALKING: DAY 1

LUDOVICO EINAUDI

Moderato ondulotorio ♩ = 78

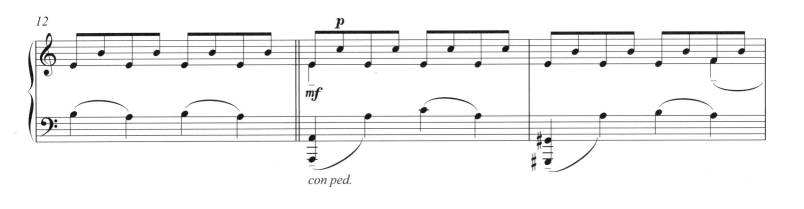

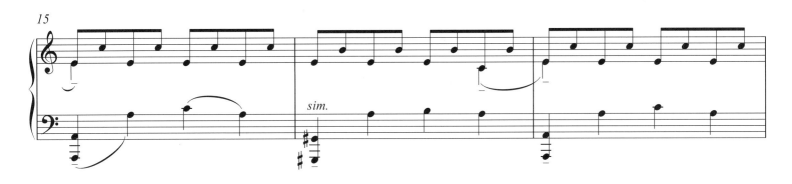

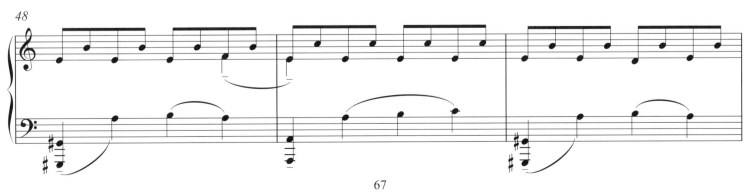

perdendosi

Ascolta

Ludovico Einaudi

Adagio misterioso ♩ = 84

Electronic effect (continues throughout)

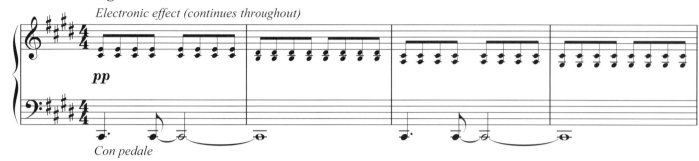

Con pedale

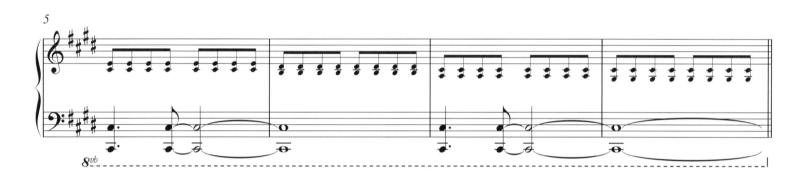

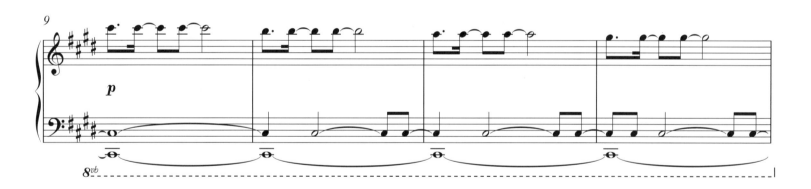

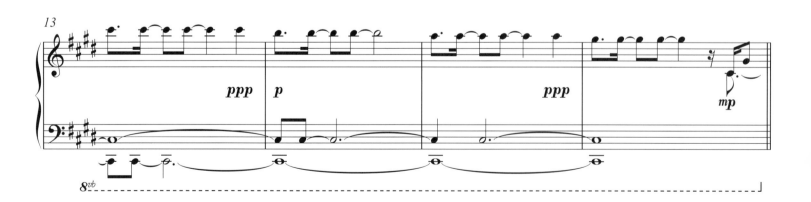

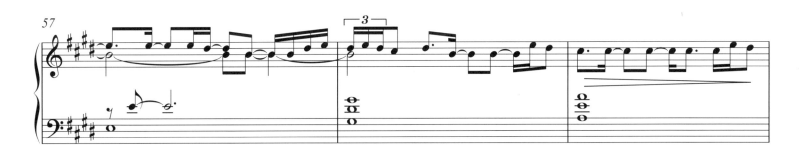

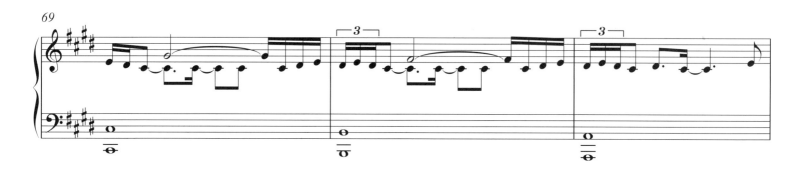

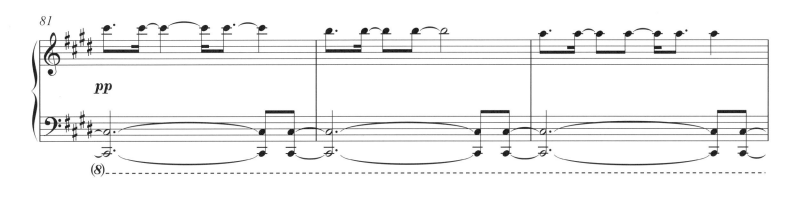

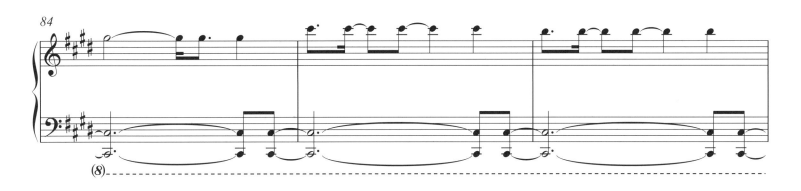

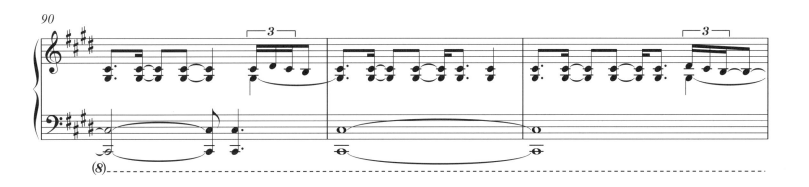

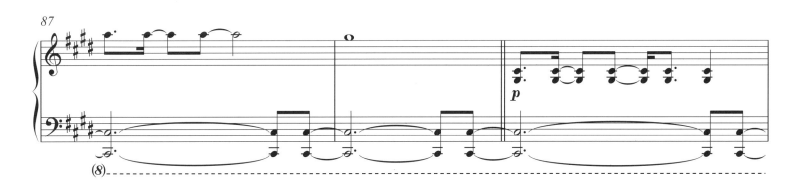

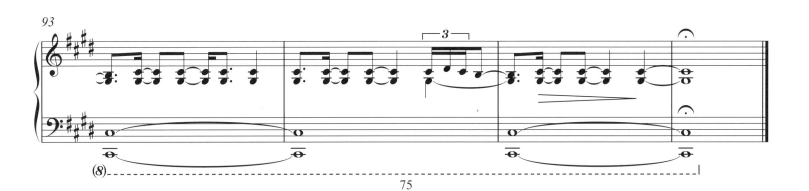

Histoire sans nom

Ludovico Einaudi

Slowly, expressively

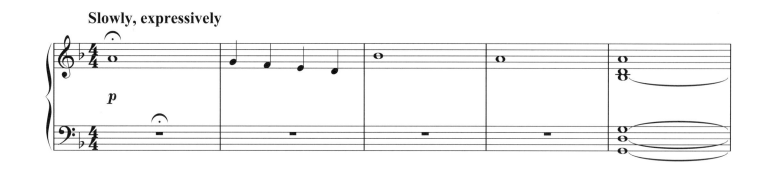

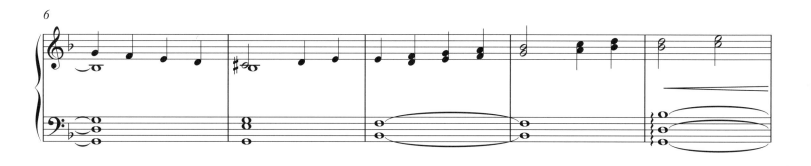

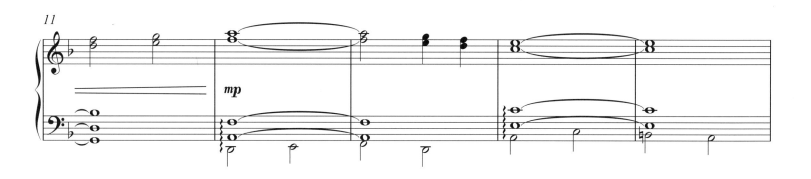

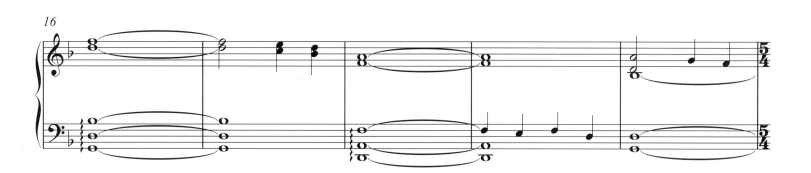

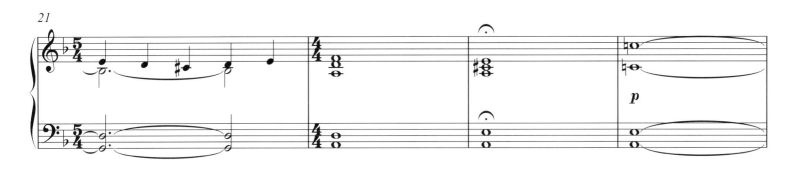

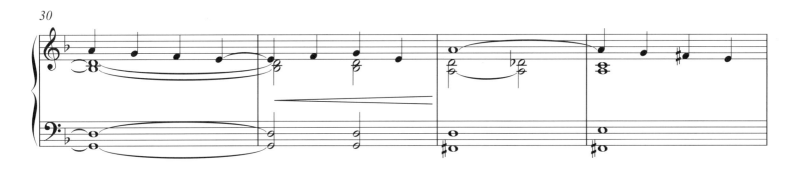

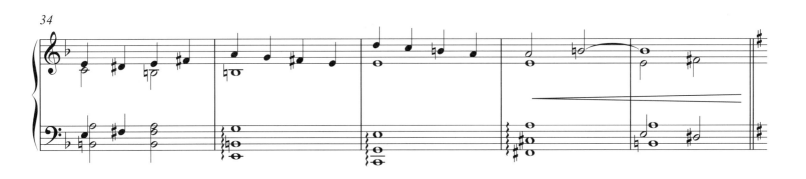

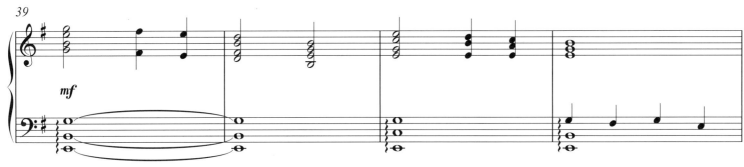

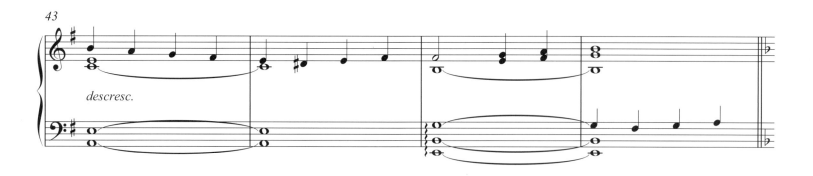

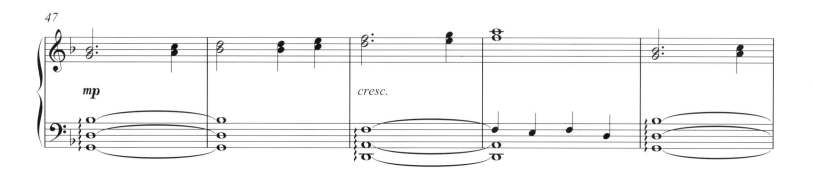

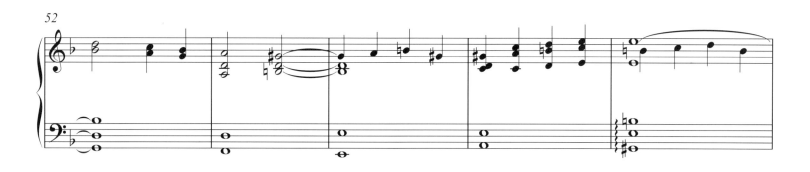

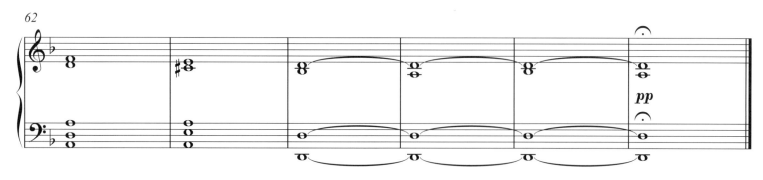

L'Origine Nascosta

Ludovico Einaudi

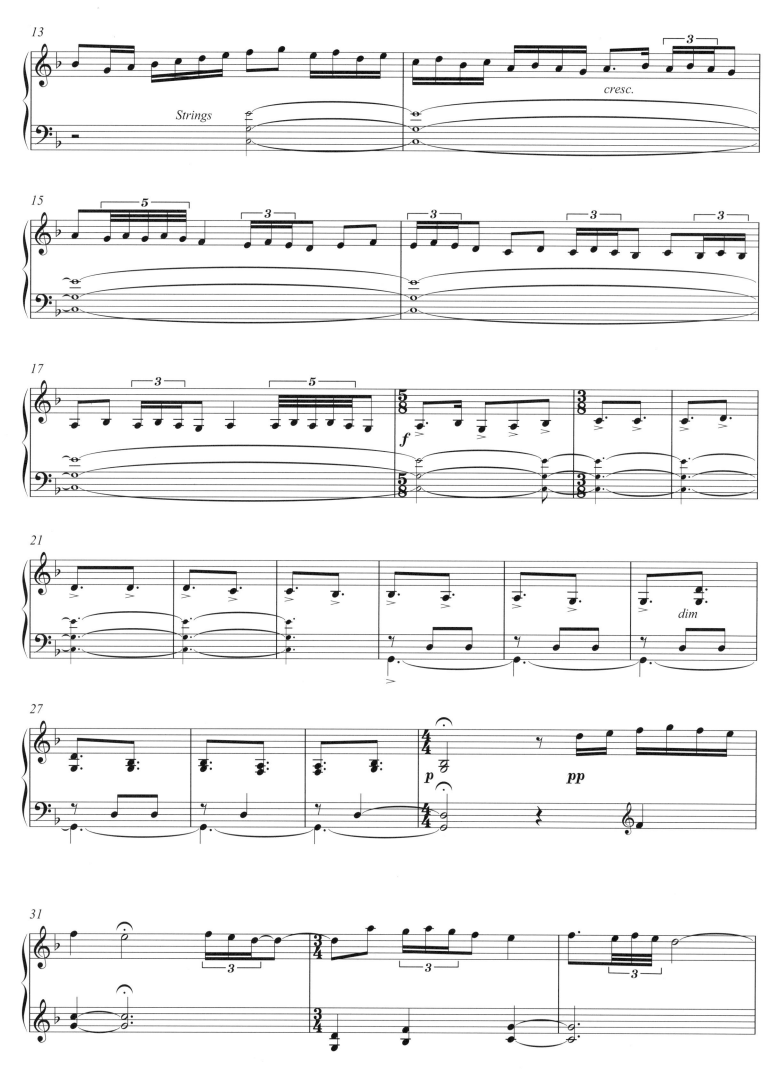

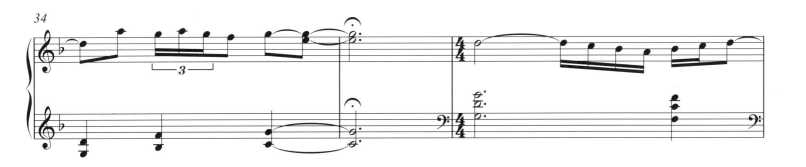

Due Tramonti

Ludovico Einaudi

Largo

sempre trattenendo un poco il canto

nobile il canto

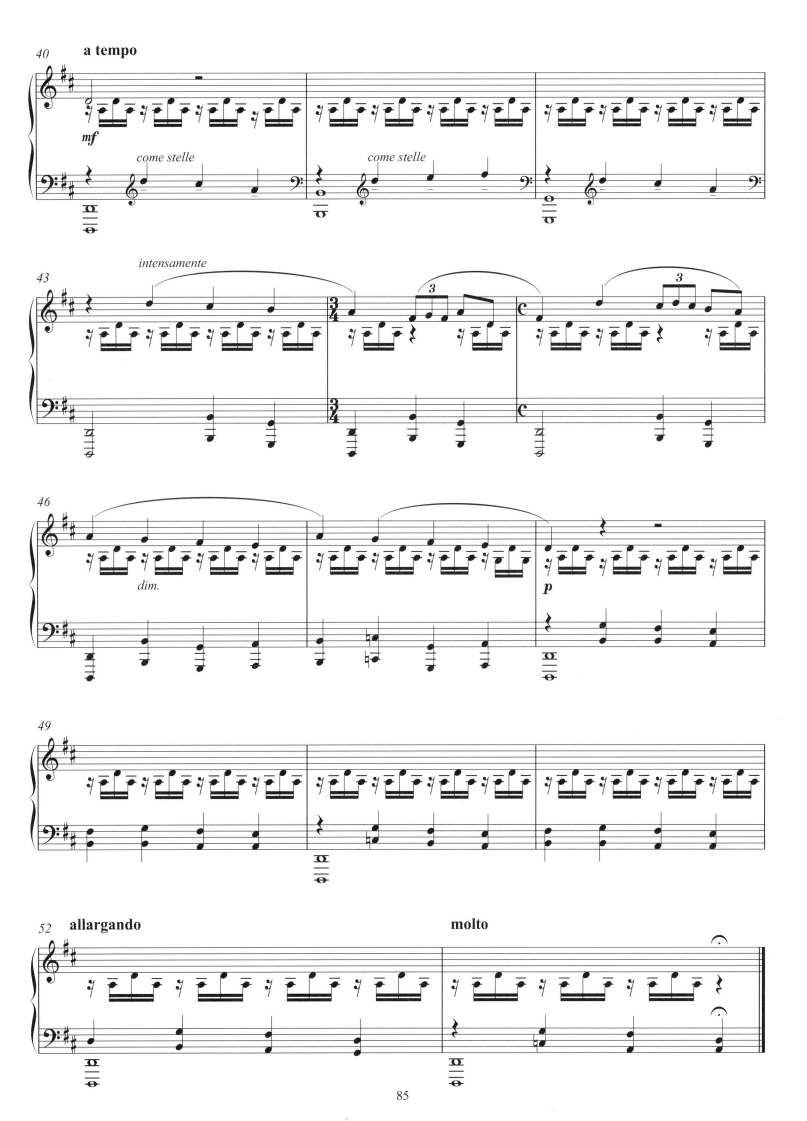

Run

Ludovico Einaudi

Le Onde

Ludovico Einaudi

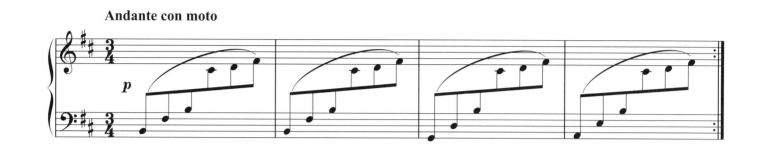

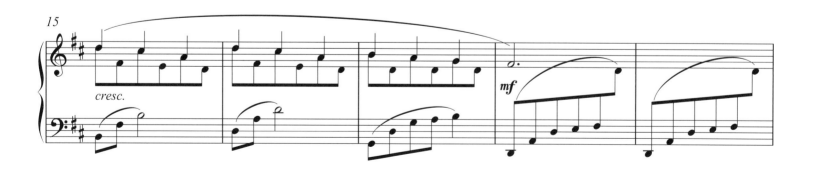

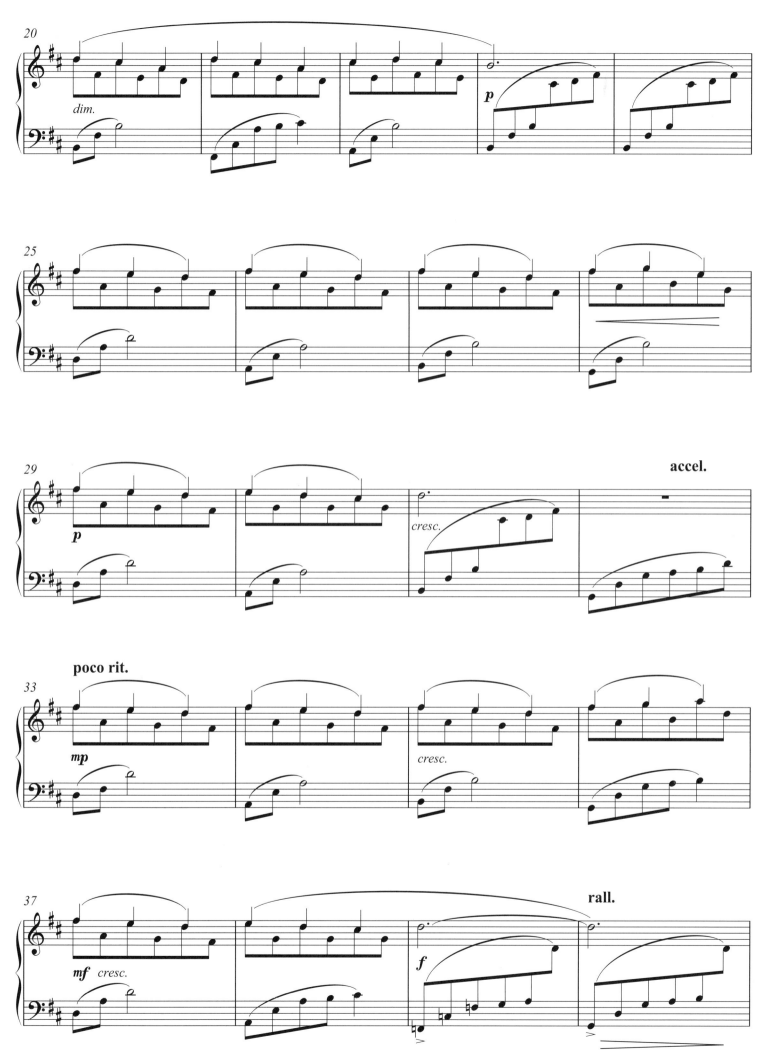

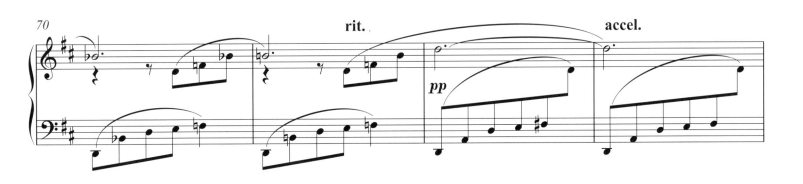

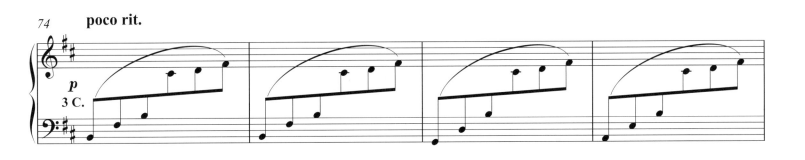

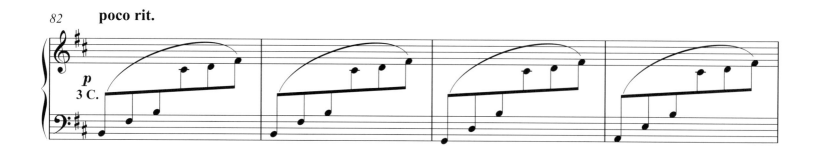

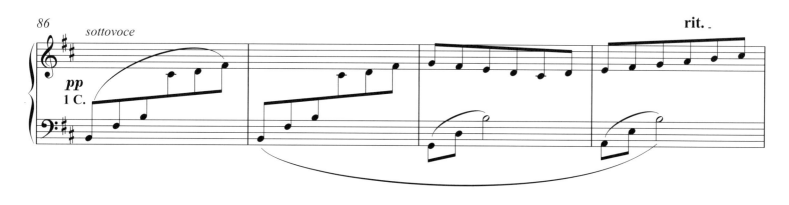

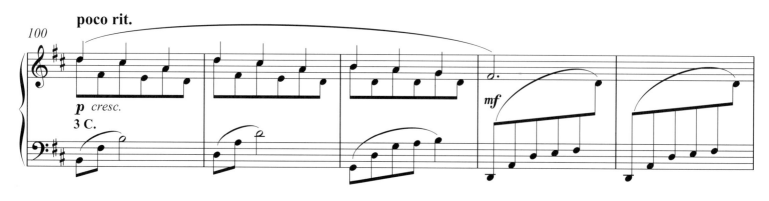

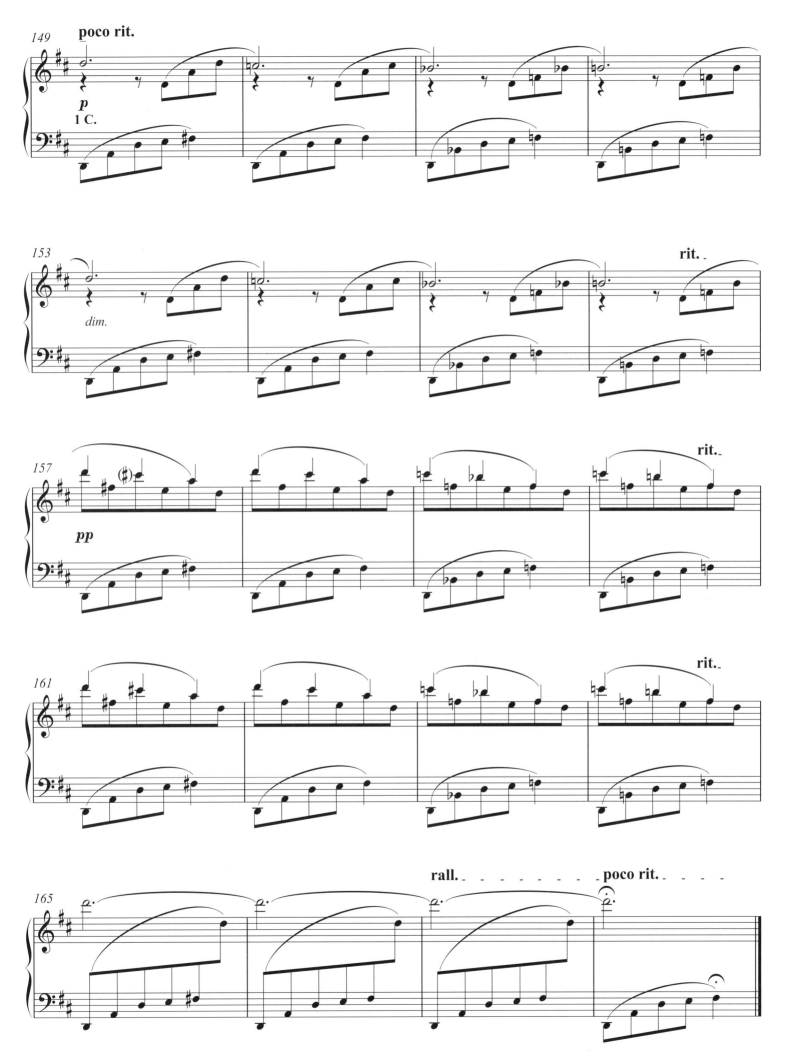